THE LONDON BOROUGH OF
BEXLEY

JOHN MERCER

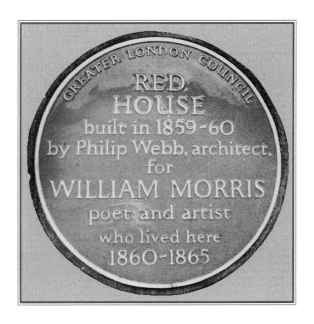

SUTTON PUBLISHING LIMITED

Sutton Publishing Limited
Phoenix Mill · Thrupp · Stroud
Gloucestershire · GL5 2BU

First published 1997

British Library Cataloguing in Publication Data
A catalogue record for this book is available from the
British Library.

ISBN 0-7509-1461-0

Typeset in 10/12 Perpetua.
Typesetting and origination by
Sutton Publishing Limited.
Printed in Great Britain by
Ebenezer Baylis, Worcester.

Hedley Mitchell's department store, Erith, in 1914, at the peak of its prosperity.

CONTENTS

Cannon & Gaze flour mill, West Street, Erith, in 1936, prior to demolition. Henry Mill is second from left in the group of four men standing in front of the building.

INTRODUCTION

The London Borough of Bexley is an amalgamation of a number of boroughs and urban districts, each of which had differing origins and developments. Bexley, Crayford, Foots Cray, North Cray and Lessness all appear in the 1086 Domesday Book. Those parishes through which the River Cray runs were essentially arable and pasture areas. The modern urban area of Sidcup was formerly heavily wooded, while Bexley Heath was covered in broom and largely deserted until enclosed in 1819. Erith developed as a river port in the reign of Henry VIII and together with Crayford became a centre of early industrialization. Ships were built, iron was manufactured and coal was imported at Erith, while textiles, iron milling, brickmaking and armaments developed in and around Crayford. The areas west of Erith were a series of heaths linking with Bexley Heath to the south and Bostall Heath on the Plumstead border. There were scattered farms, and down on the marshes, first drained by the monks of Lesnes Abbey, sheep were kept.

In the nineteenth century with the coming of the railway, Upper Belvedere (taking its name from Belvedere House) developed residentially. At the same time Bexley village and Bexleyheath, along the newly named Broadway, began to grow into larger communities, in part due to the manufacturers in Crayford, Erith and the Woolwich Arsenal. The settlements of Welling and East Wickham became residential places for the Woolwich and Erith workers. The gun at modern Welling Corner has been placed there to symbolize the relationship between Welling and the former Arsenal. The Dartford line via Sidcup, built in 1866 and the Bexleyheath line built in 1896, also opened up the districts to further housing and commercial development.

After the First World War, much of the remaining farm and heathland was built on by large-scale housing developers, and large parts of the present borough became home for London commuters. In Sidcup and Bexley a good deal of parkland belonging to the great estates has been preserved for public use, while the woods in Bostall and the grounds of the Abbey have been preserved. The green belt has protected farm and woodlands to the east of the borough, and parts of Erith and Belvedere are open spaces. Lessness marshes have been built on by electricity and heavy industry which are today being regenerated from their abandonment after the Second World War. Crayford marshes have also been heavily encroached upon by industry and housing. Most of the northern side of the borough is hoping to develop more employment as a consequence of the Thames Gateway initiative. Erith town centre appears to be the poor relation while Bexleyheath has been developed to house the Civic Centre and the main shopping area of the borough.

This selection of photographs with their explanatory captions endeavours to illustrate the multiple fortunes of the borough since the mid-nineteenth century and to capture at various points in time the variety of life to be found therein. The borough possesses a surprising wealth of historic buildings, both residential and industrial, and a rich fund of local history. There is a variety of building styles, a goodly number of noble trees, and splendid examples of parkland. Bexley should not be dismissed as a wasteland of featureless urban development. The sections cover themes such as churches, industry and schooling, across the borough, but there is an index at the back whereby the reader can see what is available for Erith or Crayford or whatever particular district is of personal interest.

Hasted's map of Belvedere.

SECTION ONE

STATELY HOMES

The area now covered by the London Borough of Bexley had a considerable number of stately homes. Many were built as country seats conveniently close to London by successful merchants and financiers. Others were built as homes for local manufacturers. Only a few have survived such as Danson, Lamorbey, Hall Place, the Hollies and Baldwyn's, and at the time of writing the last two are becoming derelict.

Blendon Hall in 1800. The estate (whose name was developed from Bladindon, after John and Mary Bladigone) dates back to the thirteenth century. This picture shows the Hall when it was built for Lady Mary Scott in 1763. The estate was broken up in 1934 and developed principally by D.C. Bowyer. Some of the magnificent trees planted by Humphrey Repton are still standing.

Foots Cray Place, Sidcup, was built in 1754 in the Palladian style for Bourchier Cleve, a London pewterer. It was subsequently the home of Benjamin Harenc, Nicholas Vansittart (1st Baron Bexley), Sir John Pender and Lord Waring. It was accidentally burned down in 1949.

Cadets of HMS *Worcester* on the east steps of Foots Cray Place. During the Second World War this house was the home of the training ship.

Howbury Moat House in 1907. This ancient defensive building lies in Slade Green and dates from the twelfth century. In 1907 the farmhouse of 1700 was still standing. Last occupied in 1935, it is now in a ruinous state. The brick bridge, built to replace the drawbridge, collapsed in 1963.

Mount Mascal was a seventeenth-century mansion built on a slope to the east of North Cray Road. The estate began to be broken up from the early nineteenth century. This photograph dates from 1947; ten years later the house was pulled down to make way for flats. This is now Jacquets Court.

Hall Place mill. Hall Place had its own farm estate and the mill which brought additional profit to its owners. Demolished in 1926, the old sluice and weir can still be seen close to an iron bridge over the River Cray behind the Jacobean barn.

Halcot, from the north, in the 1920s. This house was part of the Hall Place estate and became derelict before the Second World War. St Columba's School for Boys in Halcot Avenue now occupies the site.

The façade of May Place. This house was originally built in 1480 and altered considerably over the centuries to become a mansion. Its most famous resident was Admiral Sir Cloudsley Shovel who died at sea in 1707. It was later the home of the Barne family who gave their name to Barnes Cray and Barnehurst. The house was demolished after a fire in 1957.

The Elms, Sidcup, was the home of Charles Edward Shea, an Ulsterman, in the latter half of the nineteenth century. It was demolished in the 1930s to make way for Sidcup Hill Gardens, a group of well-designed maisonettes.

Belvedere House celebrating the coronation of King Edward VII in 1902. At that time it had become the Royal Alfred Home for Aged Seamen. The house was originally built in 1740 and in 1847 was acquired by Sir Culling Eardley who was largely responsible for the development of the Belvedere area. In 1920 the eastern part of the estate became Franks Park. The last remains were demolished in the early 1980s.

The Hollies, Sidcup. This house was built for the Lewin family in about 1852, adjacent to a demolished Tudor house, Marrowbone Hall. It later became the administrative centre for the children's homes run by the Greenwich and Deptford Board of Guardians. While the other Hollies homes have been converted into modern dwellings, this house remains empty and neglected.

The south side of Danson Mansion dressed for the coronation in 1953. Built in 1768 for Sir John Boyd, it was also the home of the Beans (hence Bean Road nearby) until acquired by Bexley UDC in 1924. Neglected by successive councils, it is now being restored by English Heritage. It is now a Grade I listed building.

Danson stables. These were built *c*. 1800 to replace detached service blocks to the house. Like the Jacobean barn at Hall Place they are being restored by a brewery as a high-class restaurant and pub.

Marten's Grove, Barnehurst. One of several large houses in the Crayford/Barnehurst area, this was built in 1850 in a park embodying a variety of landscapes. Demolished in 1932, it became a municipal park with an open-air swimming pool.

The pool in Marten's Grove which was closed in 1989. Much of the estate has now been built on but a narrow, well-wooded stretch of parkland remains.

The Baldwyn's mansion is a stuccoed villa dating from 1802. It was occupied by the American inventor, Hiram Maxim, at the turn of the century. He experimented with an early flying machine in the grounds and invented the Maxim gun (see page 84). It is now part of Bexley Hospital and is becoming derelict. This photograph was taken in 1941.

Gamekeepers on the Baldwyn's park estate in about 1900.

Shenstone, off Old Road, Crayford. This house was built in about 1828 for Augustus Applegarth, the paper and textile manufacturing pioneer. It was enlarged by David Evans in the 1840s and remained in this family's ownership until 1935. The house was demolished in 1974 and Shenstone School now occupies the site.

Mr F. Burton (1895–1959) at work in the greenhouse at Shenstone. When the house was sold to Crayford UDC, he became a propagator for the council, working at St Stephen's Road depot in Marten's Grove in 1947.

Lamorbey Park, Sidcup, a Grade II listed building and now the home of Rose Bruford College of Speech and Drama. It was built in 1774 on the site of a much earlier house. The present style dates from the ownership of the Malcolms who resided there from 1812 until returning to Scotland in the 1850s.

Crayford House which stood opposite the Town Hall. It was pulled down in the 1950s.

The River Cray as it passes through the grounds of Hall Place. This charming picture of two village lads looking into the water was taken in 1893.

SECTION TWO

SHOPS, STREETS & HOUSES

H ouses, shops and pubs sprang up in all the local districts in the nineteenth century. Some still remain but many of the older shops have been replaced by town centres full of multiple outlets. There are some fine examples of middle-income houses still to be found but the whole area has been intensely developed for cheaper housing, most of which is owner-occupied. The bulk of the housing stock was built between the two world wars when farmland was sold to developers.

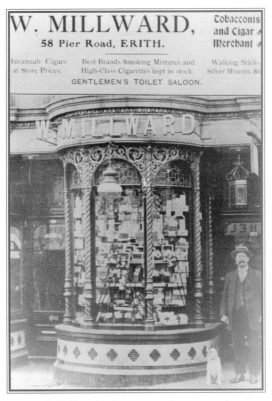

Mr W. Millward, tobacconist and cigar merchant, 58 Pier Road, Erith, pictured in about 1900 with his dog.

Woodbine Cottage, North Cray, was last used as the local general store until it was demolished in 1968 to make way for a dual carriageway. At this point Mr Peter Tester identified it as a medieval hall-house. It was dismantled, stored and then re-erected in 1978 at the Weald and Downland Open Museum, Singleton, near Chichester. It was the oldest shop in the borough.

O.O. Dale, jeweller and outfitter, 141, 143 and 151 High Street, Erith, *c.* 1914.

The Cosy Corner Café at the corner of Lion Road and Broadway, Bexleyheath, *c.* 1925. A computer shop now occupies the double site.

Patullo Higgs & Co., corn merchants at 239 The Broadway, Bexleyheath. This picture was taken in 1929. There was also a branch in Sidcup High Street until the late 1960s.

Mrs Rose, the florist, in Bexley Village in 1935. This could be from 'Happy Families'!

Barnehurst stores in 1930. This was the first shop to be opened in Barnehurst in Mayplace Road in 1928. It was owned by Mr Perrier who had nine children, five boys and four girls. It later became J's Leisure Wear.

The junction of Albert Road with Parkhurst Road, Bexley. This photograph was taken in 1951. Little has changed, except the electrical distribution box has gone, the pillar box has moved to take its place and the general store has become 'Teak Antiquity'.

Straw's Handy shop, on the north side of Broadway, Bexleyheath, in 1934. This was an amazing ironmonger's selling an incredible variety of nails, screws, glass, tools, paints and much more.

Looking towards the clock tower, Bexleyheath, in 1950. The trolley bus was then transport king as cars were few and far between. The whole area is now pedestrianized.

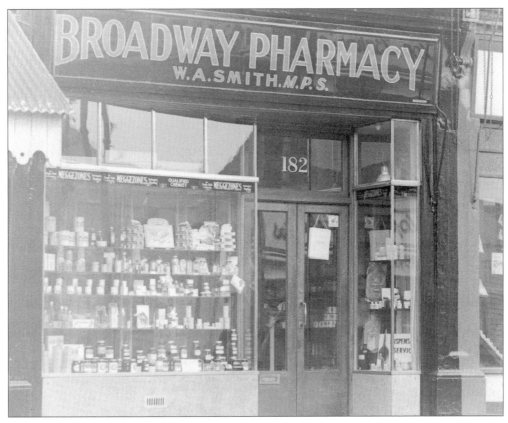

The Broadway pharmacy in 1950. It was opposite Sandford's the greengrocer's.

Mr and Mrs W.A. Smith and their daughter, Yvonne. He holds a citation as the Chairman of the Bexley Chamber of Commerce in 1955. Mr Smith was the proprietor of the Broadway pharmacy.

Demolition of property in Cross Street, Erith, in preparation for the new town centre in 1966.

The end of an era. Mitchells, 'the house of quality', boarded up and ready for demolition in 1966.

The Cross Keys on the High Street, Erith, in 1970. The pub dates from 1749 and was one of four in the London Borough that used to issue tokens in lieu of currency. Tokens were issued because of the shortage of legal currency. They could be spent only by trading with the issuing house. Burnt down in 1891, it was rebuilt in its present form a year later. The cottages next-door which survived the fire have recently been restored.

The north side of Broadway, Bexleyheath, in 1950. The entrance to Townley Road is on the right. Jennings was a popular toy shop and seller of fancy goods and prams. Its demise was deeply regretted.

Hide's department store near the clock tower. It had a wide range of goods for sale and a fine restaurant. The shops nearby included Carrier's, the baker, and Jenkins, stationers.

The area around the clock tower, Bexleyheath, was demolished to make way for the shopping mall in 1980. Townley Road can be seen at the bottom left, Woolwich Road at top centre and Mayplace Road West at the top right. The former Palace (Astor) cinema has yet to be pulled down. The curving shops opposite Pincott Road (Norwich Place) have survived, for the time being.

The Embassy Rooms in Welling. This was a popular venue for dancing and dating as well as for formal luncheons and dinners in the 1950s.

The Crook Log in 1950 before it was altered to give better accommodation for more diners. This may be the oldest pub site in the borough, dating from 1605. There was a toll gate close by to charge traffic using the Dover Road (Watling Street, later Broadway).

The Station Hotel, Welling, in 1950. It was built in 1897, two years after the Bexleyheath line was opened. It recently became the Moon and Sixpence after a £300,000 refurbishment.

In 1946 these rather disgruntled women had to queue for the rations which they are showing to the photographer. Bread rationing was introduced after the Second World War had ended, as a result of world food shortages.

Bexley High Street in 1950. Styleman Cottages are on the left and the former workhouse is in the centre by the station approach. Note the absence of traffic.

The Black Prince in 1950. Built on land belonging to Bourne Cottage when the A20 was constructed, it was upgraded into a Forte Trust House in the 1980s.

Brook Street, Erith, *c.* 1900. This is the junction of Carlton Road (left) and Parsonage Manorway (left). Highams Farm is behind the trees.

Bexley Road (Nuxley Road since 1939), Belvedere. This view was taken from the top of Picardy Road, looking across Woolwich Road to Bexley Road. The strange structure in the middle of the picture was a public urinal.

Upton Road, Bexleyheath, at the junction with Red House Lane, *c*. 1900. The lane was named after the Red House, built by Phillip Webb for William Morris and his wife in 1858.

Heron Hill, Belvedere, in 1907, also known as Herring Hill. This was the name of an ancient house which stood at the top of the steep slope.

Some fine, late Victorian houses in Warren Road, Bexleyheath, pictured in 1970. They are locally listed on account of their interesting brickwork.

Two semi-detached, mid-Victorian villas in Woolwich Road, Bexleyheath. They have now been demolished but 65–67 Albion Villas still remain and are Grade II listed buildings.

Some fine Victorian houses about to be demolished at Crook Log to make way for new, denser development in 1970. The Crook Log public house gave its name to the local area.

Two little girls are interested in a tinker under the cherry blossom in Bexley, 1943.

Building houses in the Drive, Blendon, 1934/5. This road cut through the Blendon Hall estate.

Cottages at the bottom of Sidcup Hill, of unusual medieval design but actually dating from the early 1900s. Bertha Hollamby Court now occupies the site. Bertha Hollamby Court is sheltered accommodation built by the Chislehurst and Sidcup housing association.

Adelaide House in 1909. This farmhouse was built in the hamlet of Pound Place, on the road between Foots Cray and Eltham, in the early nineteenth century and became the home of the Martins. Thomas Martin was a monumental and general mason and well known in the district. Another branch of the family had a mason's business in the Broadway next to Christchurch. This house still stands in a builders' yard close to Sidcup fire station.

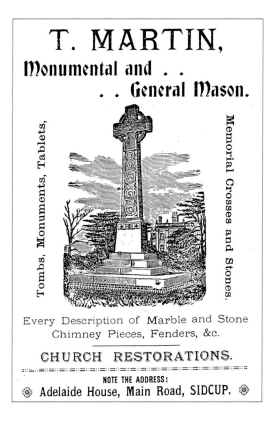

T. MARTIN,
Monumental and . .
. . General Mason.

Tombs, Monuments, Tablets,

Memorial Crosses and Stones.

Every Description of Marble and Stone
Chimney Pieces, Fenders, &c.

CHURCH RESTORATIONS.

NOTE THE ADDRESS:
❀ Adelaide House, Main Road, SIDCUP. ❀

A gathering in the garden of Red House, Red House Lane, Bexleyheath. The Red House was built for William Morris by his architect friend, Phillip Webb, in 1858. It is a Grade I listed building.

Jay's Cottages, opposite the Three Blackbirds, Blendon, date from the early eighteenth century. The pavement is now higher than the ground-floor level, as the road has been built up over the years.

Munition workers' huts at East Wickham in 1957. They were built on both sides of Upper Wickham Lane for employees of the Woolwich Arsenal during the First World War and survived until after the Second World War.

The open-air swimming pool at Danson Park opened in 1936 and was constructed by S.H. Alabaster Ltd. It was situated close to the A2 and attracted large crowds of people in the summer. It finally closed after it was vandalized in 1981.

A group of gipsies with their teachers on the Erith marshes in 1936. Gipsies camped on the marshes for over a century.

Part of the gipsy encampment on the Erith marshes. They were badly affected by flooding in 1938 and again in 1953. The 1953 floods served to hasten their departure.

Erith public library built in 1906 in the terraced garden belonging to the house of the late J. Parish. The Town Hall, built in 1931, stands where Walnut Tree House (the home of Mr Parish) once stood.

An ex-service squatter moving into an empty army hut in Crayford in 1946. Later the huts were acquired by the Urban District Council to legitimize this kind of occupation.

SECTION THREE

CHURCHES

The oldest churches in the borough are those mentioned in the 1086 Domesday Book: St Mary's, Bexley, St Paulinus, Crayford, All Saints, Foots Cray, and St James', North Cray. Later in the Middle Ages are mentioned St John's, Erith, and St Michael's, East Wickham (now the Orthodox, Christ the Saviour). As the districts grew in the nineteenth century, churches and chapels sprang up to provide places of worship for the burgeoning population.

The chapel-of-ease in Oaklands Road, Bexleyheath, was the first church on the heath. It was built in 1835 and demolished in 1877 but the tower remained standing until 1928.

The restoration of St Paulinus Church, Crayford, in 1937. From the top of the tower Richard Parry, stonemason, is teaching his son, Michael, the skills of the trade.

St John's (old church), Erith, in the snow in December 1906.

St John's, Erith. This picture was taken when the north aisle was being rebuilt during restoration work in 1877.

The Congregational Church in Avenue Road, Erith, in July 1907. It was built in 1859 and suffered war damage. Restored, it later became redundant and was demolished as part of the town centre development. Today there is a McDonalds on the site.

Christ Church and Sunday school buildings, Erith, in 1915 before the houses were built in Crescent Road and Glebe Way behind. It was erected in 1874 by James Piers St Aubyn and the tower and spire were later added in 1915.

A very mobile church! Originally St John's, this building was put up in Bourne Road, Bexley. In 1880 it was moved to Albert Road. In 1916 it was moved again to Barnes Cray and re-dedicated to All Saints. It was demolished in the 1960s.

The London City Mission, Mill Road, Northumberland Heath, in 1910.

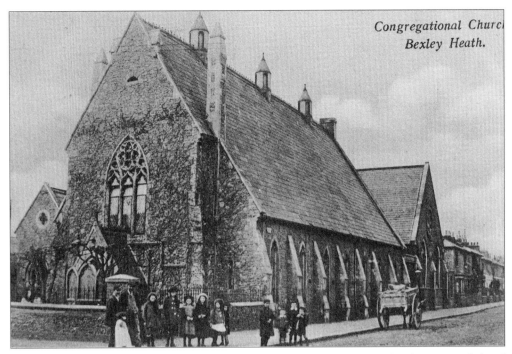

The Congregational Church, Mayplace Road West, Bexleyheath, in 1907. It stood at the corner of Chapel Road opposite the Palace (Astor) cinema.

The Revd J. Geddes, minister of the Congregational Church from 1869 until 1920. The new United Reform church in Arnsberg Way is named after him.

St Mary's Vicarage, Bexley, seen from the south. Canon J.H. Wicksteed was the vicar. It is now an old people's home, the new vicarage being in Hill Crescent, Coldblow.

The church of the Holy Redeemer, Lamorbey, in the snow. A child is taking her toy clown to the service in February 1963.

Repairing the steeple of St Mary's, Bexley, in 1905. A good head for heights is required for this job!

Tea ladies at St Paulinus church hall, Crayford, in 1964.

Bexley ladies bible class dressed for a dramatic performance in 1912.

Laying the foundations of the new Bexley Strict Baptist Chapel, Bourne Road, *c.* 1900.

The Orthodox Church of Christ the Saviour, Upper Wickham Lane, when it was still St Michael's. A new St Michael's was built close by in 1933 and became the parish church of East Wickham in the Southwark diocese.

The Bishop of Kingston, the Rt Revd F.U.T. Hawkes laying the foundation stone of St Michael's in 1933. The new housing in Stuart Road can be seen behind.

Bell-ringers at St John the Evangelist, Sidcup, in 1977. Peter Dale is at the board with Sian Davies next to him, Ruth Burston is top right with Carol Jackson standing in front of her.

Erith Salvation Army Band marching along West Street in 1924, towards St John's Church.

Laying the foundation stone at St Peter's, Pickford Lane, Bexleyheath, on 29 September 1956. Left to right: Revd P. Pavey, Dr Chavasse (Bishop of Rochester), a workman from Thomas & Edge, Lady Best-Shaw, Mr E.J. Pearce (director of Thomas & Edge), Mr A. Ford, architect, and Revd A.E. Ramsbottom (vicar).

The pantomime, *The Red Dwarf*, at St Peter's Mission Hall, Pickford Lane, in 1936. Back row, left to right: Mrs Ruth Kennerley (first left), Eva Saunders (third left), Winnie Alkins (first right), Mrs Cox, as the fairy queen is on the extreme right. On the front row are Miss Snook's little dancers from her dancing school in Pickford Lane.

SCHOOLS

In the nineteenth and early twentieth centuries there were a number of private schools all over the present borough, with a particular concentration in Sidcup and Bexleyheath to provide education for the middle classes. Church schools were built for the poor and local school boards, beginning in Erith and Crayford, were set up to cater for increased numbers of pupils. Only after the Second World War was free secondary education made available to all.

SIDCUP COLLEGE,

HEAD MASTER :
T. B. SANDERCOCK, F.C.S., M.C.P.
(Late Head Master East Devon County School. and Teignmouth Grammar School).
VICE-PRINCIPAL :
Rev. LAUD HAVARD, B.A.,
Assisted by
A. H. TOWN, B.A., R. BASSETT, HERR LACK, W. JESSOP.

EXAMINATIONS :

During the last three years pupils have been successfully prepared for the following Examinations :—Army, Navy, Responsions *(Oxford University)*, London, Dublin, and Durham University Matriculation, Law and Medical Preliminary, Oxford University Locals, College of Preceptors, Competitive Examinations for Banks, Insurance Offices, Commercial Houses and Civil Service Clerkships.

SUCCESSES OF PUPILS :

Chinese Civil Service	1
Woolwich Royal Military Academy	1
Naval Cadetship	1
Medical Preliminary	4
Law Preliminary	
Public School Scholarships, £60, £30, £20	4
Public School Entrance Examinations	8
Cambridge University Local Examination *(Honours)*	6
Oxford University Local Examination *(Fourth place in England)*	35
College of Preceptors	95
Competitive Examinations for Clerkships	8

1894—47 Boys presented for Exams. 46 passed.
1895—49 ,, ,, ,, 46 ,,
1896—12 ,, ,, ,, 11 ,, 2 honours.
1897—40 ,, ,, ,, 37 ,, 2 ,,
1898—22 ,, ,, ,, 20 ,, 3 ,,

FEES:

BOARDERS—Under 13 years of age	15 guineas per term.
,, 17 ,,	16 ,, ,,
Over 17 ,,	20 ,, ,,
WEEKLY BOARDERS	13 ,, ,,
DAY BOARDERS	8 ,, ,,
DAY PUPILS—Under 8 years of age	3 ,, ,,
,, 14 ,,	4 ,, ,,
Over 14 ,,	5 ,, ,,

These Fees are payable in advance ; either a Term's Notice or a Term's payment is required before the removal of a Pupil.

———:o:———

References and further information on application.

A 1923 advertisement for Sidcup College, a private school. This occupied Sidcup Place until the Chislehurst and Sidcup UDC acquired the empty building as offices in 1934.

Bexley National School (Church of England) was opened in 1834. This shows the school in 1951 before it was sold for industrial use. There are several small enterprises there today, including C.J. Design Partnership and the Papilio Studio.

Group Two at Bexley National School in 1905. There are twenty-five children shown – a small class for those days. Classes could be as large as sixty or seventy.

North End infants' school, Erith, was a Board School transferred to Erith Urban District in 1903 when all school boards were abolished. This shows a class in 1930.

Central School, West Street, Erith, in 1919, opposite St John's Church. It was originally built as Picardy Boys' School in 1889 (a Board School). It has now been demolished. During construction of the new Spire Road, a medieval building was uncovered where the school had been. It is thought to be the fortified manorhouse of De Luci who founded Lesnes Abbey.

Mother care class, Brook Street School, Northumberland Heath, in 1914. One wonders why this subject was ever abandoned. Miss Saunders, the teacher, is standing at the back. The class obviously learnt about care of babies.

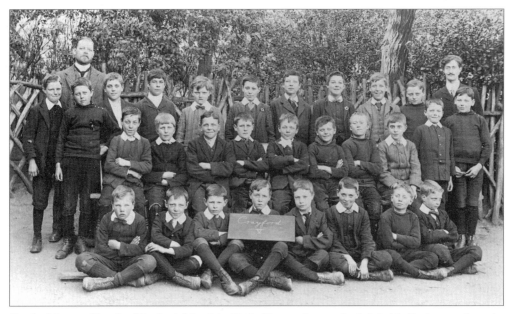

Crayford Junior Church of England School in 1915. The teacher on the left is Mr Darkson and on the right is Mr Revison, who later taught at Dartford Grammar. He became a doctor and had a surgery near Crayford Bridge. Mr Dunmall, who provided the photograph, is the pupil, fifth from the left, in the back row.

Mayville convent in 1956 shortly before its closure. It stood opposite Welling Way.

Girls of Mayville convent in 1956. Top row, left to right: Diane Taylor, Judith Jackson, Paula Ramsden, Brenda Simmonds, Glenys Johnson, Sonia Dixon, Susan Boswell, Yvonne Smith, Frances Tearle, Pat Bartholomew. Second row: Alison Murray, Sylvia Chapman, Linda Maxwell, Frances Halse, Marion Stuckey, Audrey Reen, Jean Barnet, Elizabeth Robinson, Pat Creaven, Pat Lawrie. Bottom row: Judith Chappell, Mary Brook-Rhodes, Pat Pitcher, Carol Hubbard, Gillain Creed, Judith Batson, Jean Cross, Jane Garner.

Laying the foundations of Erith Grammar School. Left to right: Mr R.T. Sumner (headmaster), Mr Andrew Bell (former head) and Mr W. Friday (builder). It was formally opened on 4 December 1954 by Dr Fisher, Archbishop of Canterbury. The builders were H. Friday & Son.

The first class of girls to attend Erith Grammar School in 1955.

Senior girls of Bexley Technical High School for Girls in 1947 with the headmistress, Mrs D. Collins, OBE.

Bexleyheath School for Girls 1st XI Hockey Team in 1960.

Uplands School, Bexleyheath, 1910. It was originally a Board School, then a Central School and is now a primary school.

A class of Uplands School, *c.* 1890. The two girls on the bottom row to the left are Lucy Hardy and Nelly Hardy. The rest are unknown.

Days Lane Primary School, Blackfen, in 1935. The children are playing team games.

Pupils of Lessness Heath Primary drinking their one third of a pint of milk in their newly built school in 1951. This was a time when spacious school buildings were built of solid materials.

St Joseph's Convent, Woolwich Road, Bostall, *c.* 1914. It is a mid-nineteenth century Italianate building acquired by the Congregation of the Daughters of Jesus in 1904. It became St Joseph's in 1905. The school closed in 1979 and the site became part of Bexley College.

Girls of St Joseph's playing netball in 1969. Two of the former pupils became very well known in the media, Jan Leeming and Kate Bush.

Picardy School for Boys champion football team in 1925.

The opening of Bexley Grammar School on 5 July 1957. On the left of the front row is Dr Chavasse, Bishop of Rochester. In the centre, behind the flowers, is Lord Hailsham, the Minister of Education.

In 1965 the headteacher of Foots Cray Church of England School, Mrs Oblath, retired. Helping her celebrate here are Dr Say (Bishop of Rochester), Councillor Ernest Reader (last chairman of Chislehurst and Sidcup UDC), the rector of All Saints, the Revd E.E. Turner and assorted pupils.

The final day at Foots Cray School, 23 July 1982. The school was re-opened several years later as the Harenc School, a private preparatory establishment for boys, named after a previous owner of Foots Cray Place.

Girls playing leapfrog, Pelham Junior School, Bexleyheath, in 1971. The school was built on the land of Pelham Farm in the early 1930s.

SECTION FIVE

AGRICULTURE

T raditionally the Bexley area produced fruit and vegetables for the London market. There were strawberry fields in Sidcup (and hops for the local breweries), cabbage fields in East Wickham and intensive market gardening in Bexleyheath and Welling. The area was self-supporting in milk production. After the First World War the large farms in Bexleyheath, East Wickham and Welling were sold for housing. Bostall Woods, Lesnes Abbey Woods to the west, and Joydens Wood to the east, survive as ancient remnants of the extensive forests of the early Middle Ages.

A dene hole found in Bexley. Many were located in
Cavey Spring off Vicarage Road.

A dene hole in Crayford, 1935. Dene holes were dug in the thirteenth century, and again in the eighteenth century, for chalk which was used to marl the stiff clay soils during periods of agricultural expansion. All known ones have now been filled in (there is one open, but fenced off in Chalk Wood, North Cray). Many new home-owners in the Joydens Wood area were surprised and alarmed to find gaping holes in the gardens (or even worse, under the foundations) after periods of heavy rain.

A dairy at Belvedere at the foot of Nuxley Road, *c.* 1915. It was owned by the Edwards family.

Briggs Dairy, Bellegrove, Welling, in the 1930s.

Mitchell & Co., Lesney Farm, Erith, in 1912. The bearded man is John Mitchell, owner, the boy in front is Stewart Heaselden, his grandson. The man with the moustache in the window is Fred Mitchell, third son of John.

The Furner Brothers nursery was situated at May Villa, Slade Green. This was the grape harvest of 1898.

Hop-pickers during the First World War. This was the King family of Bexleyheath, working on Vinson's Farm, Sidcup.

Chaff-cutting on Mitchell's farm, Avenue Road, Erith, in the 1930s.

The Gibson family at East Wickham Farm. Mr and Mrs Bruce L. Gibson and son are seen here with Nurse Ford in 1900.

The peacheries in 1953, prior to the construction of Forster's Crescent off Mayplace Road West, Bexleyheath.

Collecting butterflies in the garden of 41 Salisbury Road, Bexley, in 1933. The butterfly farm of Mr L.W. Newman, founded in 1905, supplied pupae and butterflies to many places, both home and abroad.

A local resident views with dismay the destruction of the elm trees because of Dutch Elm Disease along

North Cray Road and St James' Way, Sidcup, early 1970s.

A quiet path beside the River Shuttle in Bexley Park Wood. Much of the wood has been built on but there are still ancient hornbeam trees to be found.

Mr L.H. Newman, with a group of volunteer schoolchildren, reducing the number of large white butterflies that were plaguing the local cabbage fields in 1940.

INDUSTRY

There was an iron mill in Crayford as early as 1570 which made plates for armour, thence Iron Mill Lane. Textile printing developed under Charles Swaisland and Augustus Applegarth who printed banknotes and silks. Other Crayford industries were saw and flour milling, barge building and brick-making. Hiram Maxim introduced Vickers to Crayford and then manufactured armaments of all kinds until 1974. Erith grew, as both a local port and ship-building town. Loam was dug and exported and brickfields developed. Iron works came next and then electric cables. Vickers manufactured armaments, and Frasers & Chalmers produced mining equipment. Most of the heavy industries had been established by 1894.

The pumping engine at Crayford waterworks, Station Road, c. 1920s.

The old mill at Bexley in the 1930s. Originally a flour mill, it became a manufacturer of sacks. After a fire in 1966 it was rebuilt as a restaurant. There was a mill of similar appearance in Foots Cray. Both are mentioned in Domesday Book.

The David Evans factory in 1930, showing Bexley House, an eighteenth-century building demolished
c. 1980. The factory is now an industrial park incorporating the David Evans works, a leading silk printer
in Europe. It was here that Applegarth established his paper and silk printing works in 1826. He built
Shenstone for his private residence (see page 16) and had extensive land on both sides of Bourne Road and
at Barnes Cray for bleaching. David Evans, a city silk merchant, acquired the estate in 1843.

The Crayford tannery of the Murgatroyd Brothers in 1951, shortly before its demolition. Older residents of Crayford will recall the penetrating odour that came from the tannery. Most of the skins processed here came from New Zealand.

The weir next to the tannery. Running water has always held a fascination for small boys — and indeed for some older ones too!

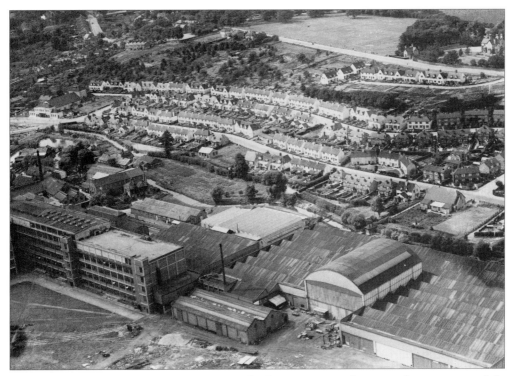

An aerial view of Vickers, Crayford, in 1929. The former Princes Theatre can be seen, centre left. Crayford Way, Green Walk and Iron Mill Lane are all in the centre.

Crayford High Street meets Old Road at the One Bell public house.

A Vickers aeroplane, made at Crayford in 1919. Alcock and Brown were the first to cross the Atlantic in one of these machines.

Trying out the Maxim machine-gun. The German Emperor, Kaiser Wilhelm II, said of this weapon: 'This is the gun: there is no other'.

Edward Butler, an apprentice engineer, took out a patent for a 'petroleum motor tricycle'. He tried out his machine in Erith in 1889.

Dussek Bros & Co. Ltd, Crayford, manufacturers of putty and oils in 1938. Here Mr G. Barton and Mr J. Gould are standing by their delivery lorry.

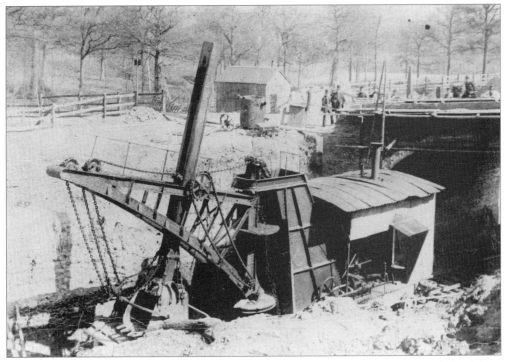

A steam 'navvy' digging out a railway cutting after heavy snow at Barnehurst on the Bexleyheath line, c. 1900.

The beam engine house of the Crossness sewage treatment works. It was built in 1865 by Sir Joseph Bazalgette in an Italian–Romanesque style and is currently being restored by the Crossness Engine's Trust, a voluntary body. It is classified as a Grade I listed building.

Two of the massive beam engines, each 12.8 m long. These were built by James Watt & Co. of Birmingham and are the largest surviving examples in Europe. They have not been in regular use since 1914.

Clarke's coal crane at the Erith Deep Wharf in 1914. Frank Clarke was the MP for Erith and Crayford between the wars. He was also a prominent coal importer and distributor. Currently, the Deep Wharf area is being developed with a new housing estate, shops and leisure facilities.

Car breaking developed as a local industry in the 1930s, especially in Erith and Lower Belvedere.

Early torpedoes being made at the Shuttleworth factory at Anchor Bay, *c.* 1880. Note the houses of Wheatley Terrace in the background.

British Fibrocrete works in 1934. Behind this runs Manor Road and on the former brickfields the houses of Apperfield Road, Springfield Road and Alexander Road can be seen. Behind them runs the railway and on the top right the former Congregational Church (see page 46) can be spotted at the bottom of Avenue Road.

Employees of Cory & Sons in 1903. These are men from the sidings shop. Cory's were coal importers, barge and tug owners. They are still involved in the power industry.

Workers at Cannon & Gaze flour mill in 1918. Back row: Ethel Martin (first left), Annie Taylor (third left), Alice Dalton (fourth left). Front row: extreme right, Ruth Sims and next to her, Gladys Stone (Mrs Durrant).

Stone's boat yard near Erith police station, *c.* 1905. Notice the single female employee and the cat!

The Gilder family both caught and sold shrimps locally. In 1912 William Gilder was head of the family and had a shrimp shop at 32 High Street, Erith, close to the Cross Keys public house.

The demolition of Cannon & Gaze mill after the fire of 1936. The river was very busy in those days.

A view of the coaling jetty at Erith Deep Wharf seen through the derelict flour mill. Since 1967 the wharf has been owned by Associated Newspapers but has not been used since 1989.

The new town centre at Erith under construction in 1972. The Odeon cinema can be seen at the top right.

Brick-making in Erith, south of Manor Road, before the First World War. Erith bricks were transported by river to build Lambeth Town Hall and Scotland Yard, among other well-known buildings.

TRANSPORT

Methods and the volume of transport developed quickly in the nineteenth century. The river was used in conjunction with the railway to move the materials of Erith and Crayford heavy industries. Trams, trolley buses, passenger trains, cars and lorries have cumulatively led to our current dependence upon quick transport. Before the tram and train those without private horse-drawn vehicles walked, some workers tramping many miles daily to work and back.

Erith pier and hotel in 1853. For nearly twenty years Erith enjoyed a reputation as a waterside resort, until the Crossness sewage works, 3 miles upstream, destroyed its pleasantness. The proposed redevelopment of the Deep Wharf (where the hotel was earlier located) may bring a new waterside interest to Erith, especially since the sewage is to be incinerated at Crossness.

Erith police station and pier, *c.* 1960. The coal wharf can be seen clearly to the right. This stretch of the Thames is called Erith Reach. The London Borough of Havering lies on the opposite bank. The former police station is now being transformed into luxury flats.

The Causeway, Erith, in 1900. Riverside Gardens opened here in 1937 and, now recently redesigned, have replaced the old, open riverside.

A view of the river frontage in 1930. Under the boom of the ship at anchor can be seen the Cross Keys pub. Erith police station lies behind the prow of the ship with the spire of Christchurch to the immediate right. The Victorian flour mills of Cannon & Gaze loom up in the centre. Behind the tugs at anchor lies the site of the Tudor Naval dockyard, occupied in the late nineteenth century by the Thames saw mills and later by a company called Venesta, which made plywood products.

Station Road, Belvedere, was badly flooded in February 1953. Here, road transport comes to the rescue.

Crabtree Manor Way, Erith, during the floods of 1953. Water transport comes into its own in a situation such as this.

Cunard liner SS *Mauretania* on her way to the King George V dock in 1939. It was the largest passenger ship ever to sail so far up-river. The ship was scrapped in 1965.

The Royal yacht *Britannia* moving downstream on the occasion of Princess Margaret's wedding on 4 May 1960.

Erith station in 1876 with a down train waiting. The Greenwich–Erith–Dartford line was the first railway in the district. Erith station was opened in 1848.

Barnehurst station when it was first opened in 1896. This was the last line to be constructed across the borough. Alfred Bean of Danson Park was the entrepreneur.

A well-posed picture of the bridge over the railway at Barnehurst station, *c*.1910. The area was nicknamed 'hills and hollows'. Soon houses grew up here and a new town was formed.

Laying the track when the railway was electrified in 1924.

A school party boarding a train at Sidcup station in 1935.

A two-tier train that ran for a decade or more on local lines. Designed to carry more passengers per carriage, these were unpopular with travellers and train staff alike as it took longer to alight and climb aboard, thus increasing journey time. Introduced in the 1950s, they were phased out by the end of the 1960s.

The first tram to run from Northumberland Heath to Erith. Until amalgamation of the Erith and Bexley tramways, passengers from Bexleyheath to Erith had to alight at Northumberland Heath and change on to an Erith-bound tram.

Erith Road, Barnehurst, in 1905. Bursted Wood is on the right. The tram tracks were single and trams had to wait and meet at double tracks which were at intervals along the road.

Tram and tricycle delivery at the market-place, Bexleyheath, 1908. The Pincott Memorial occupies the place now taken up by the clock tower. The market house can be seen in the centre of the photograph, with the grocer's Penney, Son & Parker behind.

An early steam bus at the King's Head, Bexley, in 1913. Its destination is Oxford Street.

A 410 bus, AEC, with solid tyres in Bexley High Street, *c*. 1930. Mrs Winifred Mann's mother is alighting from the bus and her father, in the trilby, is awaiting her. AEC stood for Amalgamated Engineering Company at Southall, Middlesex, bus manufacturer.

Disaster has struck! A Cannon & Gaze steam lorry crashed at Crayford Bridge on 22 November 1907. A policeman narrowly escaped death.

Tram meets trolley bus in 1935. The old is giving way to the new.

Buses from Sidcup garage on dispersal as a precaution in case the garage was bombed, winter 1943. The children seem to be on their way to school in Oxford Road.

Courtesy cops on the Sidcup bypass in 1937. They are warning and advising motorists about the junction of the A20 with Chislehurst Road. Today the traffic at this spot is continuous with the construction of the overpass and underpass.

Another crash! This time a lorry has jackknifed into a cottage in West Street, Erith, c. 1970.

WARTIME

T he borough was in the path of German bombers, VIs and V2s, aiming for London and sometimes for local targets. These are the casualties as recorded from September 1939 until May 1945.

LOCAL AUTHORITY	KILLED	WOUNDED
Bexley Borough	155	2,050
Chislehurst and Sidcup UDC	178	1,537
Crayford UDC	66	485
Erith Borough	109	1,381

Canon Sydney Groom surveys the damage done by a flying bomb (V1) to Holy Trinity Church, Lamorbey, in 1944.

A direct hit on an Anderson shelter. The three people shown are standing on the spot where their Anderson was before it received a direct hit by a high explosive bomb. They escaped with minor injuries.

Terrace houses in Albert Road, Belvedere, badly damaged in 1941. Twelve houses, shops and a public house were damaged beyond repair. Flats have been built on the site.

Burndept's factory in West Street, completely burned out by incendiary bombs dropped on the night of 19 April 1941. The premises were rebuilt after the war and for some years they manufactured electrical goods. The site is now occupied by blocks of flats.

The milkman carries on, bombs or no bombs. Bill Phipps of Lamorbey Close, Sidcup, with his milk boy, Wally Scarboro of Hurst Road (then aged eleven), delivering milk in Pinewood Avenue in 1940. The horse was called Princess.

The bombing of Fraser & Chalmers in Fraser Road. Originally an American firm, it was established in Erith in 1891 and manufactured steam plant, milling machinery and other heavy engineering goods. A trading estate now occupies the site.

The discovery of an unexploded bomb in Highland Road, Bexleyheath, while developing the Civic Centre,
c. 1980, many years after it was dropped. There are still a number of UXBs in and around London.

Some of Crayford ARP personnel in 1940. Tom Critchley of Barnehurst is on the extreme right. His helmet denotes that he was a stretcher-bearer. The man on the extreme left was a post warden, judging by his white helmet. Few of these would have been paid for their work as most were voluntary workers.

SECTION NINE

PEOPLE

Selecting people for this section has proved a difficult task. It is hoped that those presented here cover a wide period of time and occupational range and are truly representative.

Mr Jeffries, winner of the Doggett coat and badge in 1909. He is wearing the Erith coat and badge. The race was founded in 1715 by Thomas Doggett, an actor. It is a sculling race for watermen in their first year after completing their apprenticeship.

Mr and Mrs John James Barton, proprietors of the Gentleman's Boarding School, Hall Place, 1860.

Mrs Pettegrove of Pettegrove's Fair which used to visit East Wickham and Welling at the end of the nineteenth century. The usual site was Lodge Hill.

Mr W.J. Hook, dressed in the uniform of the Bexleyheath Temperance Band. After serving in the Boer War he emigrated to Canada. His grandfather farmed in Hook Lane and gave his name to the road.

Mr E.S. Cope in his Home Guard uniform. He was managing director of Hedley Mitchell's of Erith.

Little Red Riding Hood and the Wolf produced at the King's Hall, Sidcup, in 1898. First on the left, with a white bow in her hair, is believed to be Grace Martin (born 1887) of the Martins of Adelaide House (see page 38).

The golden wedding of Thomas and Thirza Martin on 9 May 1924. Back row, left to right: Herbert T. Martin, Joseph C. Martin, Edward G. Vine. Second row: Lily Brown, Doris Martin, Ethel Martin, Bertha Martin, Anne D. Martin, unknown, Olive M. Martin, Winifred Martin, Dorothy Brown, Grace Vines (née Martin). Seated row: Rose Martin, Rhoda (sister of Thirze), Thomas and Thirza, Alice and Ebeneezer Joseph. On ground: Ronald Martin, Christine Vines, Margaret Martin, Andrew Brown, Margaret Vines Walker.

Roy Dwight, a native of Belvedere, at his Chievely Parade sweet shop in 1966. He played outside right for Nottingham Forest when they won the cup final in 1959. He scored one of the goals.

Sir Edward Heath and Councillor Raymond Pope, mayor, granted freedom of the borough in 1971. Here they are inspecting air cadets.

Alan Knott, another native of Belvedere. He joined the KCC in 1964 and became one of England's most famous wicket-keepers.

The late Peter Tester FSA leading a tour around Lesnes Abbey. Mr Tester was a schoolmaster and an authority on local archaeology and history.

Bexley Chamber of Commerce Annual Dinner at the Embassy Rooms in 1955. Mr and Mrs Smith (second and third left) are at the top table. See page 25 for a picture of their pharmacy.

The singer Joan Regan at her wedding to Dr Emmanuel Cowan on 12 September 1966 at Caxton Hall. Dr Cowan had a surgery in Station Road, Sidcup. The little girl on the right is Donna, Joan Regan's daughter by a previous marriage.

H. Robinson Cleaver at the organ of the Regal cinema, Bexleyheath, in 1935.

Opening the new turbine shop at Fraser & Chalmers in 1955. The mayor of Erith, Councillor Mrs H. Jerome, BEM is meeting Lord Citrine (on extreme left) at the station. The town clerk, in robes, is J.A. Crampton, and the mace bearer is F. Good.

The Archbishop of Southwark, the Most Revd Monseignor Cyril Conrad Cowdrey (a native of Sidcup) at the prizegiving of St Mary and St Joseph in Sidcup in 1966. Left to right: Revd C.A. Howarth (headmaster), J. Madders, M. Gannon (head boy), Canon J. Crowley (chairman of governors), the Archbishop, P.M. Lawrence, J.H. Arlisa and J. Hopkins.

ACKNOWLEDGEMENTS

I would like to thank Stuart Bligh, Frances Sweeney and Sue Barclay of the Local Studies Centre for the use of many photographs and for their unfailing help. I would also like to thank Topham Picture Point for permission to reproduce twenty-three photographs and Aerofilms for permission to reproduce two. I have been able to use several photographs belonging to the Bexley Civic Society and in my possession. Thanks are also due to Mrs Yvonne Wright and Miss Christine Vines for some of their family photographs. Finally I thank John Prichard and Russell and Elizabeth Gray for help in editing.

INDEX